Poor Boddy

Written by Leonie Bennett

Illustrated by Julie Park

On Monday,
Bobby didn't want to get up.

3

He didn't want his breakfast.

He didn't want to go to school.

He was hot and he was tired.

Poor Bobby was ill.

Bobby went back to bed.

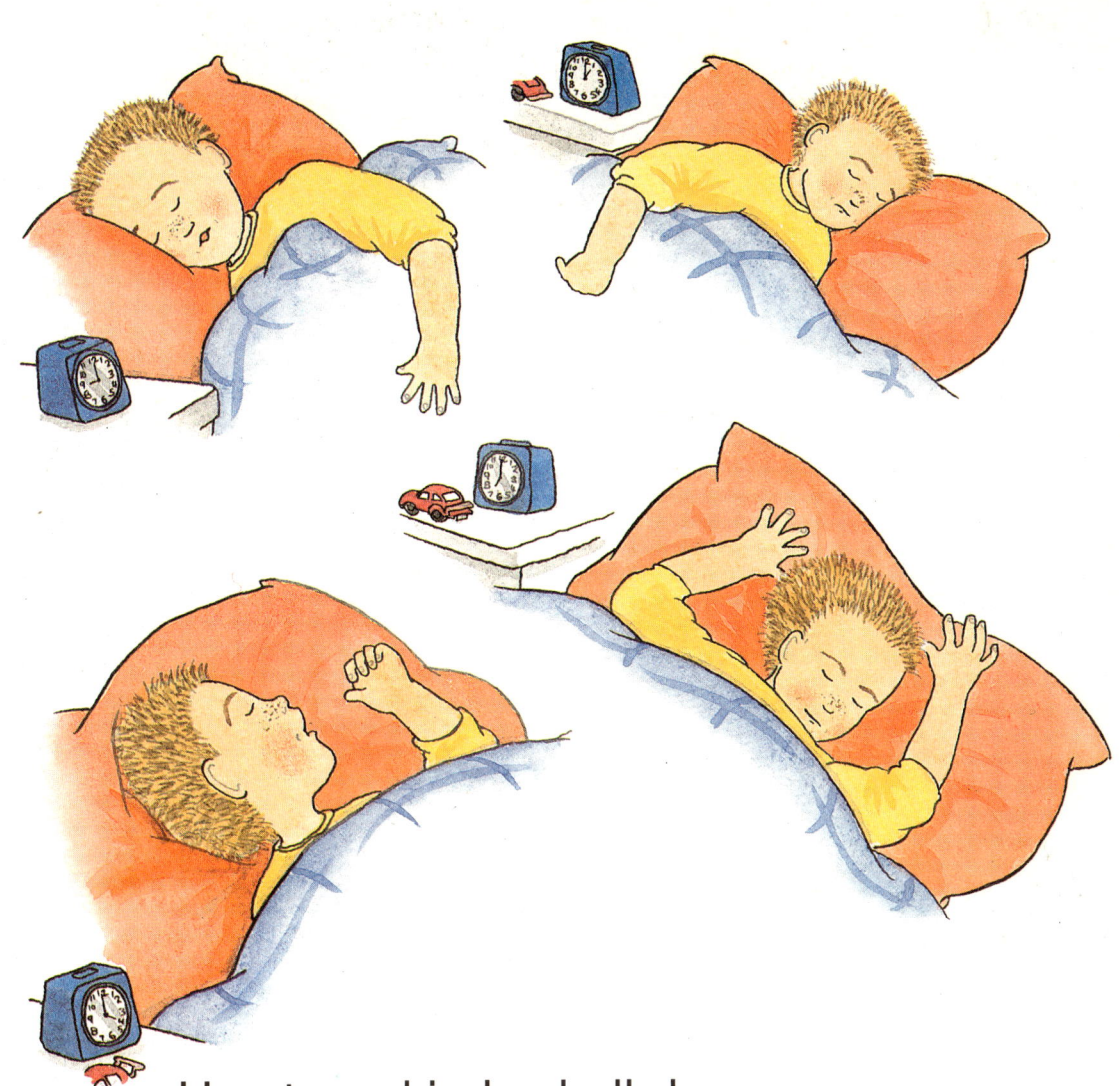

He stayed in bed all day.

On Tuesday,
he wanted to get up.

He wanted to watch TV.

On Wednesday,
he wanted to watch TV and
he wanted his breakfast.

On Thursday,
he wanted to play with his cars.

On Friday,
he wanted to play with his cars and
he wanted to play football . . .

15

But he **still** didn't want to
go to school.